Lola & Sophie's ABC Adventure

Written by
Christine Devane

LIL SMITH
A Division of Silversmith Press
Houston, Texas

Copyright © Christine Devane
Starr Photography by Suzanne Merrill

All rights reserved.

This book, nor parts thereof, may be reproduced in any form by any means without written permission from the publisher, except for brief passages for purposes of reviews.

The views and opinions expressed herein belong to the author and do not necessarily represent those of the publisher.

ISBN 978-1-967386-43-7 (Softcover)
978-1-967386-46-8 (Hardcover)

Dedication:

This book is first and foremost dedicated to Lola and Sophie. They are the two best dogs anyone could have ever asked for. I hope Lola is happy in heaven knowing that she is in a book.

To my family for always supporting me, attending my events, being my biggest cheerleaders and listening to my ideas - my parents Joyce and Tony, my husband and children, John, Joey, Nick and Adeline, my brothers Anthony and Eddie, my in-laws Dee Dee and Pops and my wonderful friends- you know who you are.

In Loving Memory of my grandparents Eddie and Ginger for always encouraging me and instilling a love of reading.

Also thank you to all the wonderful people who selflessly spend their time and energy rescuing animals, especially **Animal Rescue Kingdom** who saved Sophie and **the Boston MSCPA** where I used to volunteer.

Follow Lola and Sophie on a doggy adventure to learn your ABC's.
Woof, woof—let's go!

A is for **a**dopted and **a**dored by a new family.

 is for barking and being quiet.

 is for car rides and chihuahua.

D is for dirty digger and dainty doggy.

E is for "Eeek!" and escape.

F is for funny and fabulous.

G is for gold gown and green grass.

H is for **h**appy and **h**elpful.

I is for **i**ce cream and **i**n the sun.

J is for jumping and just sitting.

K is for kisses—kids love them!

L is for lovable little Lola and lovable loud Sophie.

M is for mini-sized and mid-sized.

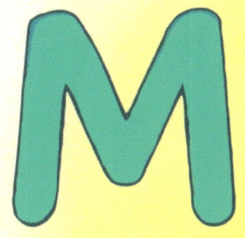

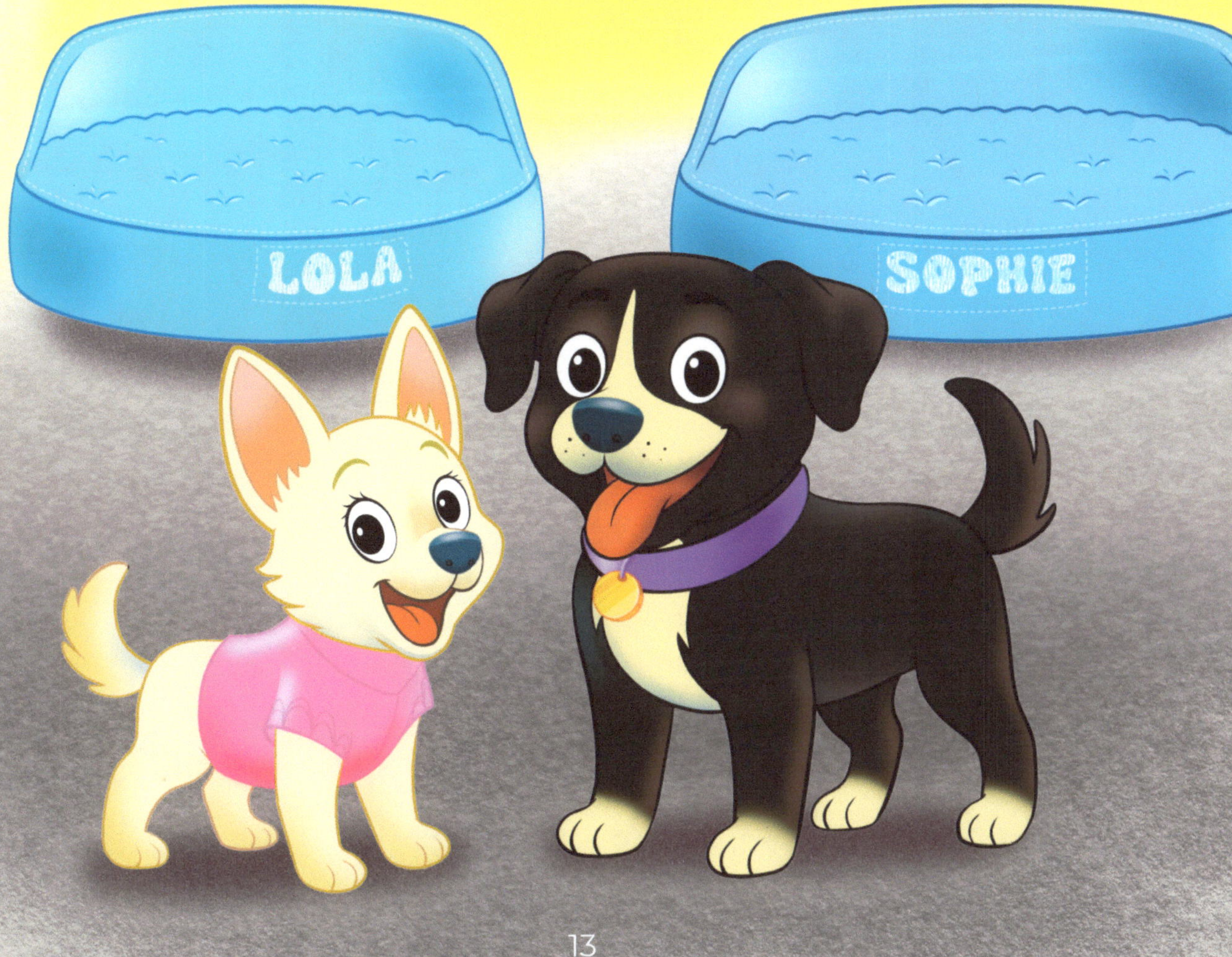

 is for naughty and nice.

 is for owner and oops!

 is for playful and posing.

 is for quack, quack and queen.

R is for rescued and "Ruff, ruff!"

S is for snoring loudly and sleeping silently.

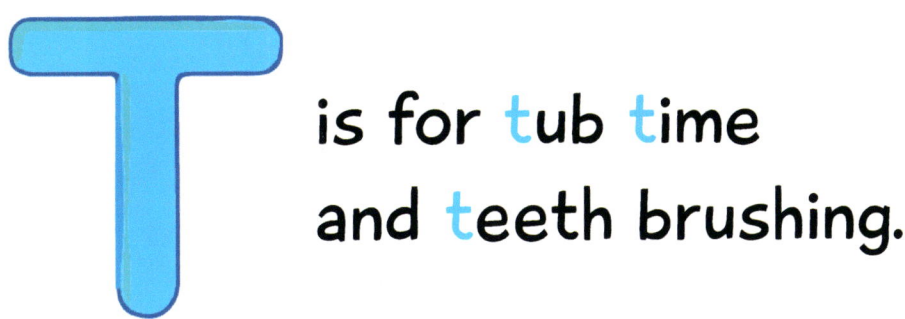 is for tub time
and teeth brushing.

 is for umbrella and underwater.

 is for violet van
and vet visit.

 is for wagging tails
and wiggly butts!

 is for x-ray and XOXO!

Y is for **y**ipping and **y**apping!

Z is for catching **zzzzz**s.

Lola and Sophie had a busy day!

Sophie's Story

Sophie was a homeless dog found on the street in Texas by animal control. She was brought to a crowded, high-kill shelter. Thankfully the kind people at Animal Rescue Kingdom rescued her and a few other dogs from the shelter, that faced being euthanized due to lack of space. Sophie then began her long journey on a truck from Texas to Rhode Island with hundreds of other dogs, driven by a nice man named Carlos. When the truck reached Rhode Island Christine and John, who adopted her online before the truck arrived, were there to greet her with a sparkly new collar, lots of love and plenty of treats. Since then, Sophie has enjoyed living in her new house and has welcomed the arrival of her human siblings- Joey, Nick and Adeline. She likes her belly rubs, going for car rides and occasionally getting into trouble. She is very loved, lucky and happy in her house but wants others to remember adoption is important.

Lola's Life

Lola and her friend Diego were purchased by Christine and her friend Allie when they were in college. The two dogs were tiny chihuahua puppies when they arrived, weighing 3 pounds each. The dogs were best friends and enjoyed playing with each other and snuggling. Lola loved her outfits, sparkly collar and being carried around. She would wait, especially in the winter, to be dressed before going outside. When Christine started teaching Lola lived with her parents- Joyce and Tony nearby. There Lola received many treats, toys and time to snuggle. She was a social dog that enjoyed being the center of attention and barely barked. She lived a long and happy life, but unfortunately in 2017 she passed away. "Lola and Sophie never met in real life, but this book is how I imagine their life together would have been." Lola's spirit and funny personality still live on, especially through this book!

About the Author-by Sophie

My mom Christine was a second-grade teacher for thirteen years and enjoyed reading with her students. She has been an avid animal lover from a young age with Lola and me being her favorite pets of course. She now lives in Massachusetts with my other humans- her husband John, and her children, Joey, Nick and Adeline. We love going for family vacations to the beach, going for walks, and snuggling up for a movie (Pets being my favorite). Christine's first book is "Elephant Beach."

www.ingramcontent.com/pod-product-compliance
Lightning Source LLC
LaVergne TN
LVHW072127070426
835512LV00002B/34